UNDERSTANDING THE CHAKRAS

UNDERSTANDING THE CHAKRAS

Discovering and using the energy of your
seven vital force centres

by

Peter Rendel, M.A. (Cantab.)

THE AQUARIAN PRESS

This edition 1990
First published as *Introduction to the Chakras* 1974

British Library Cataloguing in Publication Data

Rendel, Peter
Understanding the chakras: discovering and using the
energy of your seven vital force centres.
1. Chakras
I. Title
181. 45

ISBN 1-85538-009-9

*The Aquarian Press is part of the Thorsons Publishing
Group, Wellingborough, Northamptonshire, NN8 2RQ,
England*

Printed in Great Britain by William Collins, Sons & Co. Ltd,
Glasgow

1 3 5 7 9 10 8 6 4 2

CONTENTS

The veil of Isis sevenfold
To him as gauze shall be,
Wherethrough, clear-eyed, he shall behold
The Ancient Mystery

INTRODUCTION

This book is written for the student who has already done a certain amount of yoga and meditation practice and wants to move forward into a deeper understanding of the principles which underlie this fascinating and rewarding subject. We feel that in view of the explosion in popularity of the subject of yoga in recent years many people will shortly, if they do not already, fall into this category.

The aim of yoga is the expansion of human consciousness so that it is eventually identified with universal consciousness. This is to be achieved by a realization of the ultimate spiritual principle within ourselves; that which is above the physical and mental and is in fact our own true Eternal Self.

To achieve this one must learn to recognize these different principles or levels within oneself; in other words learn to distinguish the finer from the grosser. Therefore one must learn to work with and control the energies in oneself. Eventually one comes to realize that all Life, including oneself, is just energy in different states or in different rates of vibration. These energies in one's own system are what the chakras are all about. The chakras are the vital force centres at the different levels of experience or consciousness in the human system.

The word *chakra* means a wheel in Sanskrit and these centres of energy may be seen as wheels or vortices of force. The energies seated at these levels manifest through these vital force centres.

This book is intended for the essentially practical student who is prepared to discover deeper realities within himself. An academic or mental understanding of a thing is not the same as actually experiencing it although it may precede that experience. No one else can know something for you any more than he can eat your food for you. These realizations can therefore only be attained by one's own efforts.

The man who sets out to discover these truths must be a spiritual adventurer. He must have the attitude of the explorer: the urge to discover new worlds and new dimensions within; the desire to explore inner space; the perseverance to succeed in his quest.

This book presents the subject not only from the traditional Eastern viewpoint but also attempts to reconcile with it the Western mystery teaching which comes down to us through such traditions as the Qabalah, hermeticism, alchemy and astrology. It is not always easy to see the whole pattern of a subject underlying its many different facets and presentations but we hope the pattern may be somewhat clarified in this presentation of the subject.

Chapters One to Six explain the occult anatomy of man. Here the structure of man's system is outlined and the magnetic polarities and energy fields are explained as they relate to the flow of vitality and the seven chakras of his system. These are the very essence of his whole being.

Chapters Seven to Nine deal with the application of these principles in practice through yoga and self training. However, these principles need not necessarily only be termed yoga. Throughout the centuries mystics and seekers have followed these same principles under numerous other names and whatever name suits an individual best is the right one for him providing it embodies the true principles.

Finally, Chapter Ten traces the relationship between astrology and the chakras. Some ideas concerning the zodiac and the planets are also considered in relation to them.

In this field of study the *modus operandi* should be:

(a) Recognizing
(b) Controlling
(c) Using

(a) To learn to recognize the principles involved and the energies which constitute the system.
(b) To learn to use these energies within oneself.
(c) To learn to use these energies creatively and unselfishly in Life.

We feel that the reader who follows these rules will gain a greater insight into life and will be richly rewarded by a deeper knowledge of himself.

CHAPTER ONE

THE BASIC POLARITY

In order to understand the chakras or vital force centres and how they relate to each other and to the whole of one's being, one must first begin by studying how the essential polarities of Spirit and Matter come into existence.

The Trinity

Any manifestation that takes place must result in a polarity or duality; if such a polarity does not occur then there can be no manifestation. The relationship between these two poles is the third aspect of the Trinity.

To prove this point, let us take any simple action as an example and see how the principle applies. Suppose the reader now says to himself 'I will close this book', in doing this he manifests an activity and thus brings into being a polarity of subject and object. The subject is 'I', the object 'the book', and the relationship between them 'will close' is the verb. If the reader should consider that this is merely playing with words let him try to think of any action that does not fall into these three parts and he will find that this is impossible.

Thus in the manifesting of any activity this threefold division is inevitably and inescapably produced and nothing can actually happen or take place in the world of name and form which does not take this triple form. This is the Trinity which is fundamental to so many religions and metaphysical systems and philosophies of the world, such as the Christian Trinity and the three gunas of Hinduism.

Names for this polarity are numerous, and we are accustomed to such terms as: Life and Form; Spirit and Matter; Perceiver and Perceived; Self and Not Self. We also use the terms Unity and Diversity because the subject or perceiver is always one whereas the objective or perceived side of life is always diverse. This is often represented by the symbol of the wheel.

If we consider the subject, verb and object aspects of the Trinity to be 'I am that', then the 'I' or perceiver at the centre of the wheel is one, but as manifestation occurs and life moves out from that central point into its objective form, diversity must inevitably come about. Thus at the rim of the wheel the spokes must be separate but at the centre they must be one. Therefore in its objective form, life will involve relationship and separation and all that goes with this: such as cause and effect, time and the law of becoming, birth, death and rebirth. This is the

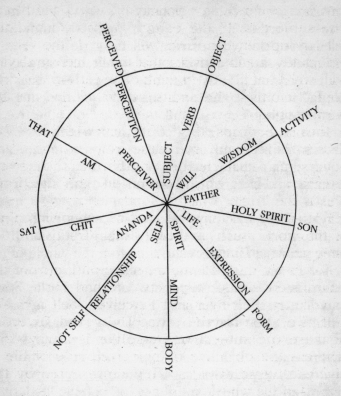

objective aspect of 'I am that'; whereas at the subjective level there is only the consciousness of pure 'I am' with no objective side. Therefore there is no experience of change, time, separation, relationship and those aspects of the objective side of life.

It is not difficult to think of numerous other terms used for this essential polarity such as Good and Evil or God and Devil, depending upon the religious or metaphysical system concerned. There can be no complete system of metaphysics or science of life which does not include this polarity. The Chinese terminology for these polarities has an especial merit as the words Yin and Yang express through their actual sounds the principles they define. Yin is essentially a subjective sound whereas Yang is an objective one. These sounds are reflected in the English words 'spirit' and 'matter' also involving the narrow or subjective *i* and the broad or objective *a*. Also in the words 'this' and 'that' which likewise express subject and object. The words 'thin' and 'fat' have similar characteristics — the fine subjective *i* having a higher rate of vibration than the broad objective *a*.

Naturally any experience in order to have a significance must have two poles or possibilities between which it can occur; therefore the whole of life is really the varied experiences resulting from the interplay or relationship between these poles. One may illustrate this by a simple example such as that of a game or sport played by two players or teams. If one of the two parties always won there would be no significance or worthwhile experience gained from it; or if one party always lost the same would apply. The significance of the experience of playing it derives from the open possibility of either losing or winning the game. Similarly in life, all the experience through which we grow and evolve derives from our being placed within this polarity of Spirit and Matter, Yin and Yang, Self and Not Self and the way in which this relationship plays through our consciousness. These polarities, the subjective and objective sides of our being and their combinations, permutations and intermediate stages constitute our total experience and is sometimes called the 'Dance of Yin and Yang'. We shall refer to this in more detail in later chapters.

Eastern Religions

Life, therefore, is both an upward and a downward process: flowing out from its source into manifestation and returning to its source with an added experience gained from that descent. In Christian terms, the soul returns with its harvest of experience 'Bearing its sheaves with it'. Traditional Eastern religions such as Buddhism and Hinduism are principally concerned with what one may term the withdrawal aspect of life through detachment of the spiritual principle from its involvement in the form of material aspect. These religions are mainly laying emphasis on the joy and bliss which is experienced when the soul is able to withdraw from its attachment to the personal self and achieve union with the higher spiritual principle within. The word 'personal' derives from the Latin *persona* meaning a mask and its use therefore indicates the transient or unreal nature of the lower self as being something which we put on at birth through which to express ourselves but which is not our real Self.

This union with the divine principle within us, our higher or real Self, is termed yoga in Hindu metaphysics. The word 'yoga', in fact, means union. It comes down to us in the English word 'yoke'. The Latin word *yugum* is derived from it and gives us the English word 'conjugal'.

In the Muslim religion the concept of union is expressed through the term *Islam*, meaning surrender of the lower self to the higher divine principle in oneself. Self-surrender is an essential of all mysticism, and Christianity has expressed this concept as

17

Communion or the Mystical Marriage.

Other philosophies, particularly Western ones, are more concerned with the aspect of bringing down the spiritual principle and expressing it in form through creative activity.

Neither of these is wholly right, or rather, each expresses a partial truth and so each is right only within its own limitation and both are necessary parts of the whole process of Life. Life is therefore both descent from one's source and return to it, and ideally one should balance the two processes. These two aspects may be termed magical and mystical, the path of descent being magic and the path of return mysticism.

Phases of Life

Most of us will not find it difficult to recognize types of people, either living or historical, who strongly embody one or the other of these aspects. Great spiritual teachers, yogis and saints are those on the mystical path whereas those such as social reformers and great inventors are mainly on the magical path, expressing spirit through form. We recognize too in ourselves these principles in our moods or states of consciousness which predominate at different times. At certain times we may seek solitude in deep meditation or communion with nature while at others we may feel the urge to express ourselves through creative activity at the material level, or by communication with others. Of course at the spiritual level no otherness exists so that the principle of communication no longer applies because one is experiencing oneness with *all* Life.

Our experience is a vibration between the two poles of Aloneness when at the spiritual level and Togetherness when communicating at the personal level in a group or partnership. Aloneness derives from All-one-ness which is the experience of wholeness or integration at the spiritual level.

These phases of life may correspond to age, sex and other factors, which are continually changing in emphasis according to the flow of life's becomingness. The rhythms or cycles which occur as the life force relates between Yin and Yang are of great importance to the serious student who seeks to know himself. They are sometimes referred to as the Tattwic Tides. Further reference to this will be made in a later chapter.

Men and women on the whole find it difficult to balance their lives and find the right relationship at any one time between the polarities in themselves. Life does not stand still but is a continuous flow or vibration between the poles. Therefore every moment of time brings a new relationship — a new experience and a new activity needed on the part of each person to fully live that experience.

Arthur Koestler expressed this as an apparent conflict between the principles in his essay 'The Yogi and the Commissar' as typifying spiritual and material man. Most people tend to remain at one level only; to be able to move between the two poles at will requires skill and discipline. They finally learn that the two principles are not adversaries but in reality are the closest of allies and they are able to balance, keeping their heads in the clouds and their feet on the ground, continually drawing on spirit and expressing it through form.

When one principle is pursued too strongly there is always the tendency for the energy to swing back to the other in order to balance. This explains the sudden changes which seem to occur in people's lives. For example, men and women who are disappointed in physical love often find the energies reacting from the lower levels and swinging upwards so that they become intensely spiritual, for a time at any rate. And on the other hand, men and women who push themselves too hard towards the spiritual plane often react by having the energies swing down into strong

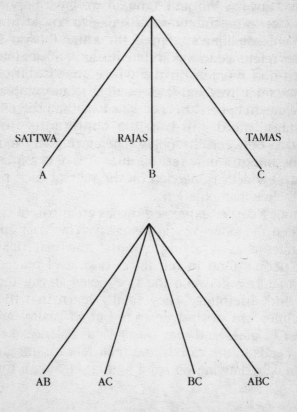

physical and material desires. The old saying 'The greater the sinner the greater the saint' or vice versa is equally true whichever way round it is expressed.

Now let us try to take these principles a stage further and see how numerologically this trinity or triplicity gives rise to the numbers 4 and 7.

From the essential or primordial unity we have seen how three must always arise in manifestation and from this triplicity a lower quaternary is born. This is so because three principles can only group themselves in four further combinations in which none of the original three is repeated. Thus if we have A, B and C these can only combine as AB, AC, BC and ABC.

The higher triplicity, 3, and the lower quaternary, 4, make 7. This is also reflected in the colour spectrum made up of three primary and four secondary colours. It is thus that mathematically and by a further stage of densification spirit descends into form and the number 7 is manifested, bringing the important sevenfold divisions in colour and sound and giving us the seven levels of consciousness in man (that is the seven chakras) with which we are now concerned.

CHAPTER TWO

THE SEVEN PRINCIPLES IN MAN

We shall now trace the way in which the sevenfold division already described in the previous chapter relates to Man. We shall see how it produces the seven levels of his consciousness and his seven centres of vital force — the chakras.

In man the essential polarity which we have discussed in Chapter One has its axis along the spinal column so that spirit has its manifestation at the crown of the head while matter (in its densest form) manifests at the root of the spine. Between these poles there are intermediate stages of consciousness, each denser than the preceding one as the life force descends down the spine in its involution into matter. One may compare this process of gradual densification with the vibratory effects which are produced in music from the string of an instrument. The deeper notes are produced as the result of the string vibrating more slowly; when the string of the instrument vibrates more quickly it produces a higher note. So it is also that the finer

THE SEVEN PRINCIPLES IN MAN

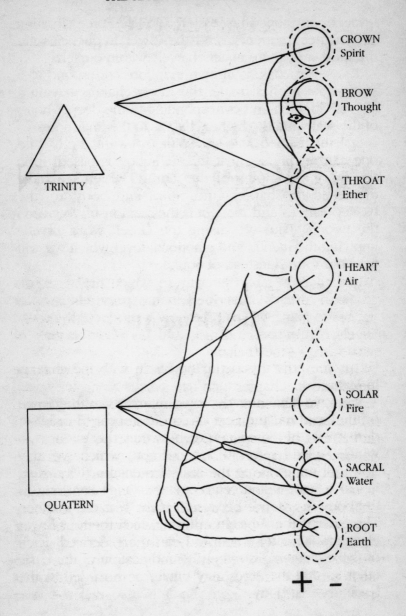

CROWN
Spirit

BROW
Thought

THROAT
Ether

HEART
Air

SOLAR
Fire

SACRAL
Water

ROOT
Earth

TRINITY

QUATERN

+ −

levels of our consciousness are the Life Force vibrating at a higher frequency, and the lower frequencies are the grosser or more material levels within ourselves.

The seven chakras in man therefore correspond to a seven-note musical scale, the lower chakras having a slower vibration and corresponding to the deeper notes of the scale and the higher chakras to the finer notes.

St Paul defined Man as 'Spirit, Soul and Body' and one can readily see that this definition is based upon the three principles of the Trinity which we have discussed in Chapter One. Spirit and body are the basic polarities and *thought* is the relationship between the two. St Paul was using the Greek word *psyche* implying the mental and emotional level which we will now term *mind* instead of Soul.

The Elements

Let us see how this definition fits in with the chakras in Man.

Spirit we have already noted manifests at the crown of the head and the next chakra to appear in order of density is the force centre between the eyebrows, which St Paul refers to as soul (but which we may now call mind) being the seat of mental activity. Next in order is the throat centre and this, as St Paul said, is the body in essence because it is the seat of the ether. The ether is the substratum from which the four lower elements, air, fire, water and earth, are derived. Each of these elements is merely a modification of the basic ether so that the ether may rightly be regarded as the basic material body.

The four elements of air, fire, water and earth have their seats respectively at the heart, solar plexus, sacral and root chakras. In this way we see that the higher triplicity and lower quaternary appear in Man strictly in accordance with the numerical laws of manifestation and the seven chakras are an exact working out of these laws.

Alchemists referred to the ether as the quintessence or fifth level of vibration and we shall see later how the four lower elements are both produced from and return to this etheric substratum or latency. The more advanced alchemists also realized that since the various levels of consciousness are merely the life force vibrating at different frequencies, it follows that one level may be transmuted into another merely by changing the rate of vibration, and hence the transformation of one element into another is a perfectly natural possibility. Through an understanding of these principles it will become possible for scientists in the future to control the weather. This also applies to the transmutation of our grosser vibrations into our finer ones. The esoteric alchemy dealt with the refinement of man's consciousness by purification until the dross of the lower self was entirely transmuted and the pure gold of spiritual consciousness was attained. This process of attainment is known under various names to all true mystics of whatever religion.

In more modern times Einstein and other well-known physicists have noted the fact that matter is thought, vibrating at a lower frequency. In earlier times alchemists performed their transmutations of one metal into another using the same principles. In fact all manifestation is merely the life force working at different rates of vibration and the difference between one element and another is merely its different frequency of vibration.

The Sequence of Involution

The body, as we have seen, is really the third or objective aspect of the trinity — that is the ether. Its four modifications comprise, air, fire, water and earth. The sequence of involution may be expressed in the following way:

For an objective manifestation to occur there must first be space within which it can do so. Therefore ether is the element of pure space alone.

Next there must be locomotion within that space and this is the element of air which is motion alone within that space.

Next there must come into being the principle of expansion which is the element of fire.

This is followed by the principle of contraction which is the element of water.

Finally the principle of solidity or cohesiveness manifests which is the element of earth.

These principles or elements are often referred to by the Sanskrit term *tattwas* meaning 'thatness' or 'suchness'. This means the essence of any quality. These elements are all that there is, in fact there is nothing else except them in the world of name or form. They are the bricks of which our total experience is built and the world of manifestation is composed solely of the elements.

CHAPTER THREE

THE FOUR POLE MAGNET

We have outlined the way in which the vertical polarity of man comes into being along the axis of the spine with its seven levels of consciousness.

In addition to this vertical polarity, man's constitution also provides a horizontal polarity. This gives a positive and negative polarity to the two sides of his body. Thus man is really a quadripolar magnet and all the laws of electricity and magnetism which are known to modern physics apply to his system.

In any system, a potential difference between two poles gives rise to a flow between them. In electrical terms this potential difference is a voltage and the amount of flow between the poles can be measured as current. Where there is a flow of current there is always a magnetic field surrounding it and at right angles to it. This law also applies to the systrem in Man: in Man there is a voltage and current between his basic polarity of crown and root. This flow gives rise to a magnetic field which surrounds him. This magnetic field is what is very often termed the aura and is visible to those who have a sufficiently sensitive and delicate sense of sight.

Thus in man's occult anatomy there are two currents of energy which flow on the right and left sides and which are positive and negative. These positive and negative currents of energy seem to cross at nodes or points between the chakras. In this way the pattern of the Caduceus or Staff or Hermes is built up. In Hindu terminology this is called the *Meru Danda*.

The Caduceus

There are several interesting features concerning this pattern of forces which we will now discuss:

Each chakra is a vortex of energy which revolves under the influence of a positive and negative

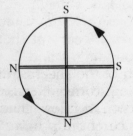

current acting upon it in just the same way as the rotor of an electric motor revolves when positive and negative electric currents are applied to it.

When the polarity of the current is reversed so that the positive and negative currents are each changed to the opposite pole, the electric motor will of course change the direction of its revolution.

An identical process takes place at each chakra.

The current flowing on one side of the body is positive and on the other is negative. As these currents cross at the nodes the positive one being dominant causes the chakra to revolve in its own direction. In effect, therefore, each chakra appears to revolve in the opposite direction to the one above and below it.

These points lead to a further conclusion based upon the laws of electricity known to modern science. A conductor placed within an electric coil through which current is flowing will conduct a current along its length in one direction. When the flow is reversed in the coil so also is the flow reversed in the conductor.

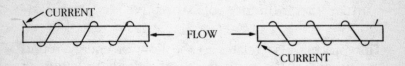

Likewise, the energy at the hub of the chakra will be outgoing or incoming according to the direction in which it is revolving. The direction of its revolution is itself determined by the influence of the positive and negative currents through the right and left sides of the body.

Alternating Currents

However, these currents are not direct but are alternating ones. Here again the alternation of the currents is a similar process to that occurring when electricity is generated. As the rotor of the dynamo revolves between the poles of the fixed magnet it cuts the lines of force first in one direction and then in the other so that a current is produced which alternates in its direction of flow. This is the alternating current which we use in our present-day electric power system.

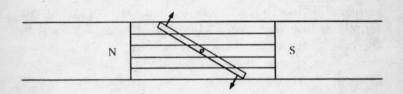

This process also relates to the flow of energy round the surface of the earth due to the diurnal rotation of the earth on its axis.

As the earth revolves between midday and midnight the current flows towards the sun, but during the other half of its revolution between midnight and midday the current (also sweeping towards the sun) will flow in the opposite direction.

Man is a microcosm of the macrocosm and this process is similarly reflected in his system. Therefore his energy currents also alternate between his polarities — north-south, east-west.

These energy currents are in fact the breath. This is the reason why the breath is of vital importance, and we deal with this in greater detail later in the book. At various times the breath predominates through one nostril or the other. The alternation of the breath in this way produces the change of direction in the flow of energy currents and the revolution of the chakras.

We have seen that each level of consciousness is a

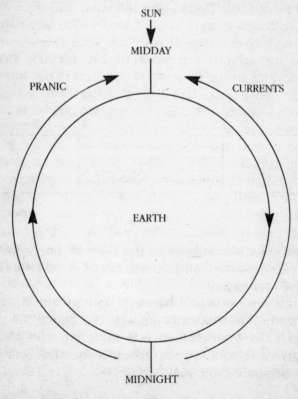

basic vibration and these vibrations are called *tattwas* in Hindu terminology. In western terms they may be called elements, temperaments or humours. As the currents flow in various ways, different tattwas or elements manifest more or less strongly in the system. Our systems, therefore, are subject to continuous change and a continuous flow of humours as one element runs its course and gives place to another. The whole principle of this flow of changing vibrations is often known as the *Tattwic Tides*.

Tattwic Tides

The flow of tattwic tides in the human system corresponds to the flow of tattwic tides in the universal system. This is the basis of the hermetic adage 'As above so below'. The flow of tattwas in the universal system manifests as the planetary influences, the signs of the zodiac and as the seasons. Within the human system too there are seasons, solar and lunar cycles and zodiacal changes in a corresponding pattern. Thus the outer and the inner life reflect each other. The tattwic tides are the working out of the periodic or cyclic law in manifestation. All manifestation is a vibration between poles as we have seen in Chapter One. The actual rhythms, the detailed courses of the flow of energies, and the different levels at which they flow are the tattwic tides. It is a fascinating thought that with a knowledge of the forces which are at work in both the universal and human systems and the directions in which they flow one is actually able to calculate the course of future events.

Ritual

It therefore follows from this that any particular activity which has to be undertaken will be more economically and therefore more effectively performed if it fits in with the prevailing energy flow — or tattwic tides — at that time and place. This is to say that there is an optimum time and place for every activity.

The art of ritual is really the magic of making use of energy to achieve a specific goal. It should be performed in accordance with the prevailing energy tides in order to achieve the most effective results. So that in the widest sense the whole of life can be lived as a ritual in which one is continually making the best of the forces which are dominant to secure the most creative results. Actions are always more effective if performed when the appropriate tattwa relative to that action is manifesting strongly. The direction in which one faces or sleeps, the colours one wears or uses at different times, and in fact every activity in life, is subject to the flow of the tattwas. The five digits of the hand relate to the ether and four elements; the thumb is ether and the four fingers (moving from the thumb) are water, earth, fire and air. By joining the thumb with the appropriate finger one creates a mudra which activates that element. This is a vast subject which we can only touch on and which it would be out of place to go into more deeply in this work.

The Sign of the Cross

One of the most widely used rituals in the Christian

world is the sign of the cross. If one makes the sign of the cross and at the same time has in mind some associations with the crucifixion, one will promote some religious feeling which may be very beneficial. But if one realizes the significance of the ritual in relation to the four pole nature of man and performs it with this knowledge in mind, it becomes a powerful ritual. As the hand touches first the brow and then the heart chakra on the vertical axis and then the two poles of the horizontal axis the effect is to balance the forces in the system. The ritual should end with a junction of the two hands in the centre and this has the effect of maintaining the equilibrium. We shall see in later chapters the practical significance of balancing the forces in relation to the expansion of cons-ciousness. It is also not generally known that the ritualistic effect of the sign of the cross may be greatly enhanced by combining it with a certain control of the breath.

One of the great conclusions that is to be drawn from this knowledge of the tattwic tides is that in the whole scheme of life every part has its proper function. One should avoid the danger of regarding any centre or level in oneself as being bad. No energy is ever bad in the *absolute* sense, but only it may be used at the wrong time or place. In other words, it may be *relatively* bad, in that it is unbalanced or maladjusted in relation to the whole. We have compared the seven levels of vibration to the musical scale. No note is bad in itself, but if played out of time and place it becomes discordant. Timing is vital, and the right note must be in the right place. We have to learn to play with all the notes in order to have whole music.

Organs of Action and Sensing

If the four poles of the human system are a fixed magnet and the chakras are the rotors, then the overall pattern is one of seven force fields caused by the quadripolar action at each chakra. As the polarities are reversed, the direction of rotation of the force fields is also reversed. The experience which we have at any of these levels will depend upon whether the energy is incoming or outgoing through that particular chakra. The outgoing energy through a chakra provides us with the organ of activity. That is to say that when the energy is outgoing we have the experience of action at that level; when the energy is incoming we have the experience of sensing at that level.

At each of the five lower chakras, therefore, we have an experience of sense which gives us our five senses. We also have five organs of action which are the same energies in their outgoing aspect.

CROWN	—	Cardinal
BROW	—	Mutable
THROAT	—	Fixed
HEART	—	Air
SOLAR	—	Fire
SACRAL	—	Water
ROOT	—	Earth

At first sight it is not very easy to understand the relationship between these organs of action and sensing. But here let us echo our introductory remarks which point out the limitations of attempted intellectual understanding alone. Through practice and self-observation one may come to realize the validity of these abstruse-seeming principles in one's own experience. More comment will be made on the qualities associated with each chakra in the following chapters.

The Middle Pillar

There is another factor of enormous significance in the human system. This is the third force which is known as the *sushumna* in Hindu terminology. The positive and negative currents are termed Pingala or Ida respectively. All manifestation gives rise to a polarity as we have seen in earlier chapters. It is when the positive and negative forces of this polarity are balanced that manifestation ceases. This third force is called the middle pillar in Qabalistic terminology. It is the channel in the centre of the spine through which the energies flow only when the other two forces are balanced. Later we shall examine the practical application of this principle more fully.

Rates of Vibration

The Indian tradition sometimes describes the chakras as lotuses and allocates a certain number of petals to each one. This notion is often confusing to the student until he realizes that this is merely another way of describing the rate of vibration or frequency of the energy at that chakra. The number of petals in each lotus is the same as the number of spokes which each wheel of force has. To illustrate this principle experiments could be made with revolving discs: these would appear to have a varying number of spokes according to the speed at which they revolve.

Similarly the colours which the chakras would throw off also depend upon the speed of their revolution. Colours are light vibrating at different frequencies. Looking at a colour will tend to produce in the viewer a corresponding vibration to that colour. By careful self-observation one may notice the level at which this vibration is seated in oneself. Each chakra has a colour relative to it and will be affected by that colour. What has been said above concerning light also applies equally to the field of sound. Each chakra has a sound relative to it and will be affected by that sound.

Starting at the root chakra and working up to the brow these vibrations are given by the Indian tradition as: 4, 6, 10, 12, 16, 2. These numbers refer to the letters of the Sanskrit alphabet. Each letter is assigned to one of the chakras and the sound or keynote of that chakra is made up of the sounds of the appropriate letters. The total is 50, the number of letters in that alphabet.

Right- and Left-Sidedness

A subject of interest which opens out from the study of these positive and negative currents is the incidence of right- and left-sidedness in people. Most people have one hand, foot or eye stronger than the other. The reason for this, in effect, is that they have either the positive outgoing or negative receptive side of their nature more highly developed at that level. It may be that in the very highly evolved person these positive and negative forces are equally balanced. It is recounted, for example, of the great adept St Germain, that he could write equally well and at the same time, with both hands.

Attraction and Repulsion

The well-known laws of attraction and repulsion in electricity and magnetism are that like repels like and opposites attract each other. These laws apply to the positive and negative currents in the human system. Sensing and acting are negative and positive. Therefore action in one person is always attracted to receptivity or sensing in another. We see this in the male-female relationship where the active outgoing male nature is paired with the receptive passive female nature.

Through the balancing or mating of two opposite poles a third quality is always born. Each new element or tattwa is formed from the interaction of the positive and negative phases of the preceding one. One may compare this process to that of stirring two ingredients together to produce a third one from their combination. Any new manifestation must always come from the interaction of a positive and negative force, as for example the incarnation of a soul through the union of male and female.

In this connection some light is thrown on the sex of children born; the relative dominance of the positive and negative factors in both mother and father at the time of conception will determine whether the incarnating soul comes in a male or female body.

CHAPTER FOUR

THE QUALITIES OF THE FIVE LOWER CHAKRAS

We shall now try to define the qualities which are associated with each of the five lower chakras, dealing with each in turn. This is to say the actual experience which we have when the energy in our system is focused at that particular chakra.

The Root Centre

The root centre is seated at the base of the spine. At this level the energies manifesting in the human system have reached their lowest rate of vibration. If we think of the energy vibration in terms of sound this would represent the deepest note as produced, for example, by the tuba or double bassoon. In fact music of these coarser vibrations such as military band music or certain kinds of jazz does produce a noticeable effect at the lowest centre and tends to produce the urge to move the feet as in marching, stamping or strutting.

As we explained earlier, the vibration of energy in the human system through a chakra produces an experience which in Hindu terminology is called a tattwa and in Western terms an element. The element of the root chakra is the quality of solidity — in other words the earth element.

The earth element gives us the quality of cohesive resistance and weight of solidness. At this level one has the experience of security and satisfaction in one's existing state and of being comfortable as one is, therefore there is no urge to move or change to another state. The earth element vibration gives one the experience of having one's feet firmly on the ground. It is a very real fact that at times when we feel insecure and nervous the vital currents are not earthed through our lowest centre.

This chakra naturally governs all that is solid in the body such as the bones, teeth and nails. The sense of smell is associated with this level. All creatures that are very close to the earth have a strong sense of smell. We also see this in people; those who are very acute in material matters very often have prominent noses.

The Sacral Centre

The sacral centre is at the level of the sacrum on the spine. At this level we have the experience of fluidity in ourselves. This is called the element of water.

The idea of energy experienced as the principle of fluidity may seem a little mystifying at first sight to the student. We have to adjust to the idea of energy in ourselves at these different levels being experienced as different kinds of consciousness or elements.

For some, the idea of ripeness or smoothness may be a more understandable way of defining the watery quality of this chakra. For example, a fruit's ripeness will require the watery element to be strongly present in it. The same thing applies to people. For man and woman to be ripe from the sexual point of view, the fluid element must be strongly present in their system. The sacral centre is thus connected with the fluid functions of the system such as the urine and the semen.

An insufficiency of the fluid element will lead naturally to aridity. This can cause hardening or drying out diseases such as arthritis. In the latter case the cartilaginous tissue which acts as a natural lubricant between the bones at the joints dries up and painful friction takes place. Ripeness and smoothness give the experience of flow, which is the fluidity of the watery tattwa.

The sense of taste is associated with this level. The English idiom speaks of the mouth watering, and it is the watery element which produces the saliva which makes this possible. The sense of taste is therefore only possible because of the element of water.

The Solar Centre

The solar centre is located on the spine at the level of the solar plexus. At this level we experience the quality of expansiveness and warmth in ourselves. This chakra therefore is the seat of the element of fire in our nature.

Fire and water seem to have in a sense opposing qualities. The smooth flow of the watery quality is downward in its direction and is therefore contractive in relation to the essentially upward expansiveness of the fiery quality.

The sense of sight is derived from the activity of this chakra. We can recognize how this comes about when we consider that sight is dependent upon light. But light is a quality of the fire element and is derived from it. Therefore the sense of seeing is only possible because of the fire element.

The strength of the fire element in ourselves at any one time will therefore govern the brightness of what we see. We can recognize the validity of this if we consider how when we are in a certain mood everything we see seems bright and strongly coloured and life seems vivid and warm. At other times we observe the world and we seem to see it as drab, colourless and lifeless. The difference between these two moods is only the relative strength of the solar chakra energy at that time.

The assimilation of food through combustion is governed by the activity of this chakra. The person who has strong vibrations at the level of the solar chakra will absorb great benefit from food he eats. The kind of person who never seems to absorb enough energy from food however much he may eat is deficient in the fire element in his system.

The Heart Centre

The heart centre is located on the spine at

aproximately the level of the breastbone. At the heart level we experience the qualities of airiness, mobility, gentleness and lightness. These qualities comprise the element of air. They are expressed as 'movement towards' and therefore as relationship or sympathy.

The sense of touch is derived from the element of air. Touch is basically the experience of relationship. We speak of being 'in touch' or 'out of touch'. This is really to say that we have more or less of the heart quality manifesting at that time. It is the air element which gives the relationship experience.

A surplus of any quality becomes a defect. This principle applies to all the chakras. At the heart level too much relationship will become oversympathy and therefore anxiety. An illustration of this point is the state that was described in Victorian days as 'having the vapours'. A surplus of the air or vaporous element in the system produced giddiness or dizziness. The remedy used was smelling salts, because smell is the sense connected with the root chakra or earth element. The energies were therefore brought down to earth and the balance in the system restored.

The Throat Centre

The throat centre is seated on the spine at the level of the throat. At this level we experience the quality of space alone. This is the characteristic of the element of ether.

We have seen that the four lower elements all have qualities which are basically activities within space: ether is the space itself within which these activities take place.

The ether or quintessence, as it was termed by alchemists, is the mixing bowl, so to speak, within which the four lower elements are formed. It is the latency behind them. It is the basis from which each element arises and to which each returns when its period of activity is ended and another element manifests in its place. The four elements are therefore really modifications of the basic ether which can turn itself into any of them. In modern radio terms the ether is the carrier wave for the four elements.

The sense of sound is derived from the element of ether. If one goes to a place where complete and absolute silence reigns and then listens intently, one will eventually become aware of a certain something which is still there behind the silence: a subtle pervasiveness which has been described as the 'noiseless sound'. When one has experienced this one has learned to recognize the etheric element in oneself; but it is more difficult than recognizing the four lower elements.

Through the ether the four elements are controlled. The throat chakra is a vital bridge between the principle of thought at the brow chakra and these four elements. This confirms the biblical dictum 'In the beginning was the Word'. Sound is the most potent of the five lower vibrations and affects them all.

The voice can take on the quality of any of the four lower elements. The voice may be heavy and unresponsive — the sort of voice one associates with solid officialdom — at the earth level. It may be ripe and sexual at the watery level, or warm and passionate at the solar level. The heart voice is gentle and sympathetic. Naturally there are combinations of these qualities and the student can learn much from studying the voice in both himself and in others.

Transmutation of the Elements

In life there is no end — only change. The sum total of energy in the universe does not diminish or increase but continuously transforms itself from one state or level of vibration to another as the flow of life manifests.

As one element comes into manifestation another one withdraws. We can observe this process going on both within and outside ourselves. If, for example, water is frozen, both the fluid and the fire element return to the ether and the solid element arises in their place. If the ice is then brought into contact with heat the solid element returns to the ether from which the fire and water have again manifested. This is really to say that these four elements are the ether which is continually changing its vibrations to manifest itself as them.

We observe these changes outside ourselves as variations in the climatic conditions. There are similar changes going on within ourselves all the time. Heat, for example, will act upon our fluidity and transform it to vapour; so as we become hot we perspire and the activity of the sacral centre is reduced. We may verify this by our own observation that after perspiring fully our sexual activity is always greatly diminished.

The elements are continually flowing in our systems as one succeeds another. However, there is in every human system always a predisposition towards one of them. That is to say that one will tend to be more influential than the others. This is due to the time of one's birth, because at that time one of the elements was predominating in the universal system or zodiac. (We deal with this in more detail in a later chapter.) So when that element is manifesting in your own system you are, so to speak, more at home: hence the saying 'to be in one's element'.

Ether, therefore, always intervenes or rather supervenes between any two of the lower elements as they change over, and it is through the throat that the lower chakras are controlled. A helpful way to understand this principle is to take the analogy of a singer. On the out-breath he will produce audible sounds which correspond to the elements. Between the notes there is a pause when he draws in breath. That pause corresponds to the ether.

Words are an inadequate medium to describe the subtle qualities of the elements. This is why most systems of teaching use symbols as an aid to recognition. For example, the Hindu tradition makes use of the qualities of certain animals for this purpose: the elephant is used as a symbol for the earth element, embodying as it does the qualities of heaviness and solidity. In many systems diagrammatic symbols are also used which are pictorial representations of the forces which have to be recognized.

Students may find it easier at first to think of the elements simply as moods in themselves. With sustained self-observation one eventually learns to recognize these levels of experience within oneself. Hippocrates, sometimes called the Father of Medicine, based his teaching on the four moods, humours or temperaments. His terminology for the temperaments of phlegmatic, choleric, sanguine and melancholic seem to be naturally related to the earth, water, fire and air tattwas of the four lower chakras.

All disease is due to the forces on the spine becoming out of balance. When the system is out of balance it is no longer whole. The word 'whole' is the same basically as the words 'heal' and 'holy'.

As the life force descends gradually into its lowest vibration at each step it involves itself more deeply into gross matter and each element is formed from the interaction of the positive and negative phases of the previous one. As each new element is formed a new sense manifests. At the etheric level only one sense exists, but at the earth level there are five senses. At the etheric level we can only hear; air, however, can be heard and felt; fire can be heard, felt and seen; water can be heard, felt, seen and tasted; and finally earth can be cognized by all five senses.

To conclude this chapter let us summarize the main points:

Element	Sense	Symbol
Earth Is content to remain where it is and does not want to move or change to any other state.	smell	▢
Water Wants to flow downwards and therefore to contract.	taste	☽

Fire   sight

Wants to expand itself
and therefore to consume.

Air   touch

Wants to move to a
different place from
where it is and therefore
to relate with something
else.

Ether   sound

Is the space within
which these four
elements operate.

CHAPTER FIVE

THE BROW CENTRE

The brow centre is located at the point on the forehead approximately between the eyebrows. The function of the brow chakra is aptly described by its Sanskrit name *Ajna*, meaning command. It is from this level, when we reach it, that we can control or command the whole personality or lower self. This is the seat of mind and at this level we experience mentation; that is to say a flow of mental images and abstract ideas continually coming and going in the mind.

The Power of Thought

Thought is so potent that it materializes itself through the ether. So that what we think, we become. Everything which exists at the material level and which is perceptible to the senses has previously been formed as a mental image in the mind of its creator.

Just as the ether is the subtle pervasive substratum of the four lower elements, so thought is the even subtler and more potent principle above the ether. To create anything it is only necessary to think it into existence. However this statement covers an enormous field of practical application and endeavour. It is very hard to bring thought under such control that it forms only those images which we want it to and no others.

The Control of Thought

The control of anything implies not only being able to use it when required but also the ability to cease using it when no longer required. If we cannot stop some process when we want to, then it really controls us, and it is not we who control it. Control of any instrument implies a certain objectivity towards it and therefore a certain independence from it. Consider the analogy of a pot of paint. If one wishes to control this and use it to colour a room one must take care not to become too involved in it. If the paint gets on one's hands then one does not perfectly control the paint. In short, one must be able to keep it at a proper distance or rather keep oneself at a proper distance from it in order to control it.

Control of thought therefore means that we only have in our minds exactly what we wish to have in the shape of ideas and images. It means that when we do not need to use the mind then we can stop thinking at will. Most people still have a long way to go before they can reach this stage and have in their minds only what they want to.

The brow centre is the seat of the third eye and the energy at this level is activated and controlled through the practice of Shiva Yoga.

Symbols

The creative power of thought may be harnessed and put to work and one of the most practical ways of doing this is through the use of symbols. A symbol is a key through which we may mentally contact a particular quality which we desire to use. It is an instrument through which we focus mentally on some quality or property which we require to work with. If for example one is feeling nervous and unstable, this will be due to a lack of the earth element in one's system. To counteract this situation and re-establish the balance of the forces one may wish to manifest the earth element in oneself. For those who are used to focusing the mind directly at the different levels this may be almost an automatic process. This process however may be greatly facilitated by the use of a symbol which represents to the user the quality of earthiness. He might use, for example, the mental picture of an elephant. By concentrating on this image he will eventually get beyond and behind the form and find that his mind is gradually assuming the quality symbolized by that form. The mind is, in fact, changing its rate of vibration and entering into the slower earth or root chakra frequency.

There will be an appropriate symbol for every quality or tattwa. However, one should be cautious of accepting any symbol as an absolute, because a symbol that represents a certain quality for one person may very well represent quite another quality to another person by its mental associations. Therefore, perhaps the ideal is to create one's own symbols. Having created the symbol be sure that it is not mentally adulterated by other associations. Its effectiveness will depend upon its purity; that is to say upon its association in the mind of the user with one quality alone.

A mental symbol can be embodied in a material form such as a statue or medallion, in which case it will become a talisman. Whereas a mental symbol will usually be individual and private to its user, a talisman may be effective independently of its creator. A talisman having been impressed with a certain mental power may be used as an instrument by others.

Telementation

By tuning in to the right mental frequency and wavelength we can communicate directly at the mental level with others no matter what distance apart. We are continually influencing others through our thought and are being influenced by them. Some of us may have had the experience of being with a person who is radiating strong positive and creative thoughts. Although no communication takes place at any other level we immediately begin to feel stimulated. Similarly with people of negative thinking patterns we feel lowered in an apparently mysterious way. Those who are unaware of what is taking place on the subtle levels of thought find these influences inexplicable and disturbing. However, when one understands the potency of the power of thought these effects are seen to be perfectly natural.

The greatest good and harm in the world is brought about by powerful thought currents operating and influencing humanity.

Time

It is activity at the mental level which gives us that experience which we call time. We have seen that in the mind there is a continuous flow of subtle elusive mental pictures as the mind enters into its modifications and transformations. Time is the sequence of these mental pictures. In other words the relationship between two mental pictures is the experience of time passing.

One may helpfully compare this to the moving pictures of a film thrown on to a screen. If firstly a picture of a rosebud is shown and then another picture of the bud opening and finally one of a rose in full bloom, one experiences a sequence of time elapsing. This is a close analogy because the mind is projecting images in the same way and as it does so we make a link or relationship between the pictures either forwards or backwards which we call future or past respectively.

The impression of time either forward into the future or backward into the past is therefore the experience of comparison at the mental level, as two related mental images or impressions are compared together.

The relationship between them is the experience of time. The vital point is that when the modifications of the mind are stilled through the concentration and meditation process there is no experience of time at all. Since images do not then arise in the mind there can be no relationship between them and therefore no time. When one is in such a state of consciousness one is aware only of an Eternal Now. As soon as the mind again begins to vibrate and produce impressions and images we establish relationships between them and once again we experience time. In terms of the illustration of the wheel used in Chapter One we have moved inwards from the rim where we experienced separateness and therefore relationship and time to the hub where there is only unity and Now.

Time, therefore, is something that we ourselves create as we produce our own mental images. These images are transient and so past and future are illusory when seen from the standpoint of the spiritual principle. This supervenes only when the mind is still.

We deal with spirit in our next chapter, but let us make a note here that one may use the mind to think about (that is to form a mental idea or concept of) spirit. Many people mistake this process of thinking about spirit for the actual realization of spirit in themselves. But spirit is above the mind altogether. Therefore, the mind deceives us with regard to spirit because the more we think about it the less we realize it.

CHAPTER SIX

THE CROWN CENTRE

The crown centre is located at the top of the head corresponding to the position of the pineal gland. It is the seat of the highest frequency of energy vibration in ourselves.

This vibration is often depicted by artists as a halo surrounding the head of highly evolved or holy people. Statues or pictures of the Buddha usually show the crown chakra at the top of the head. The tonsure practised by monks had its origin in the functioning of this centre. Christian tradition refers symbolically to the twenty-four elders who for ever cast their crowns before the throne of GOD. This also refers to the outpouring of spiritual energy through the crown centre.

The Mystical Marriage

At the mental level there is the experience of objective

thought impressions or images arising in the mind. At the spiritual level, there is only the pure subjective experience of *I am* without an objective side. In terms of the Trinity or three gunas, one has discarded or withdrawn from the second and third principles and centred oneself entirely in the first principle. When this has been done one has achieved yoga or union. The lower self has been united with the higher by transmuting the energies from the lower centres to the highest. This is the Mystical or Alchemical Marriage. In Hindu terms it is the Union of the Purusha and the Prakriti.

It is the experience which is referred to in so many of the mystical statements such as '*I am* the Way and the Light'; 'Be still and know that *I am* God'; '*I am* all things to all men'. At the spiritual level there is only the experience of *I am*, but because one has identified oneself with the spiritual or universal principle within oneself, one can speak from the universal level. One can say *I am* and know that the *I* is the whole of life because one has universalized one's consciousness.

'Lo *I* make all things new' also expresses the sense of newness, sometimes referred to as a sense of wonder, experienced at the spiritual level. It is consciousness at the crown chakra which is this experience of the indescribable bliss of union with one's own source — the divine reality within one's own consciousness. It is the mystical experience of all religions. This state has been beautifully described as one of 'isolated unity' and it is truly the experience of aloneness, But, paradoxically this aloneness is All-one-ness which is of course really the origin of the word. At this level one realizes unity with all life; in terms of the symbol of the wheel used in Chapter One, one is at the centre of life and separateness based on objective experience has disappeared. So in order to become one with all life at the spiritual level, it is another paradox that one must move away from it at the outer or personality level.

Many people do not have the courage to renounce attachment at the personal level because they feel that they are separating themselves from life. Only when this renunciation is made does one realize that the only thing one has given up, in fact, is the illusory limitation of the lower self. In doing so one emerges into a higher realm where one is closer to all beings in a unity of a deeper and more real nature. In order to find one's true self one must give up one's lower or illusory self. This finding of the true self corresponds to the transmutation of the energies from the lower chakras to the crown.

Time, which we have seen is the experience of relating mental images to each other as the mind produces thought forms, does not exist at the spiritual level where all is *now* and yet at the time ever new.

Reality and Illusion

In terms of Vedanta the spiritual experience is Advaita or non-duality, because the objective polarity of life ceases so long as one is centred in the subjective Self. Can one remain eternally in this high state? Here we come to one of the subtlest metaphysical questions that can ever be debated. Seen from the standpoint of the time world there is a continuous vibration or rhythm between the poles of spirit and matter and therefore we cannot stay in spirit any more than we can stay asleep all the time. We must always experience the rhythm of sleeping and waking, of inbreathing and outbreathing, birth and death, and all the pairs of opposites which go with the objective world of time and form. It is these rhythms which give us the tattwic tides which is the same thing as the cyclic or periodic law in all manifestation.

Anyone who has meditated will know that he cannot remain for ever in meditation, but after he has contacted the higher levels within he will eventually have to bring these down and express them through creative activity in manifestation. When this expression has been completed he will feel the urge to again return into himself. The bliss of union with the divine principle within is perhaps as relative as any other experience in that its significance lies only in relation to the opposite state — objective duality. Water is only delightful to drink to someone who is dry, heat to one who is cold, and cold to one who is hot.

But looked at from the standpoint of the spirit, can one not say that in reality one never leaves it? This seems to be the traditional Vedanta viewpoint: that the objective world is Maya or illusory in that nothing in it lasts but its forms are continuously appearing and dissolving like the waves of the sea. Only the *I am* consciousness is eternal and changeless.

However, can one not say that even an illusion is real to someone at the time he experiences it? In the Indian parable of the rope and the snake a man mistakes a piece of rope for a snake and is afraid. When he realizes that it is a rope his fear disappears. In fact it was an illusion because it never was a snake. But is it really true to say that it never was a snake? To the experiencer of the illusion its snakeness was perhaps as real at the time as the subsequent experience of it being a rope. The problem when solved appears simple, but for someone who has solved it to keep telling those who have not that it is simple may not be very wise. If someone asks you the way to Hyde Park Corner and you reply that when he gets there he won't need to know the way you are refusing to admit that two standpoints can exist.

CHAPTER SEVEN

BREATH AND THE CHAKRAS

The human breath may be defined as the life force ebbing and flowing between the vertical polarity of spirit and matter (crown and root) and the horizontal polarity of the right and left sides in the human system.

The Great Breath

In the widest sense one speaks of the great breath as being the ebb and flow of the life force between the polarities in the universal system. In fact there is a correspondence between the human or microcosmic energy system and the universal or macrocosmic energy system. One is a reflection of the other and this truth is embodied in the ancient hermetic saying 'as above so below'.

The universal or great breath includes the movement of the planets and heavenly bodies in their periodic cycles, and the signs of the zodiac and the seasons. The human breath similarly has its cycles and seasonal flows. The activities of the chakras correspond to planetary cycles as the planets work through them.

The human breath is not, however, attuned to the great breath in the lives of most people. This alignment or attunement of the human breath with the great breath is a goal which we have to achieve and represents the complete identification of the personal self with the universal self.

The Rhythm of Breath

The keynote of the breath is flow, and the rhythm of breath in the human system is one of rising and falling of the energies. The fact seems to be seldom fully realized that with the in-breath the energy is drawn upwards to the higher chakras, whilst with the out-breath the energies flow downwards into the world of the senses. Thus, in the literal sense, in-breath is aspiration which takes us upwards into the realm of spirit and out-breath takes us downwards into matter.

Therefore it follows that when we wish to make an effort which involves bringing energy into manifestation on the downward impulse, we should always initially take a deep in-breath. When the lungs are full, the effort itself should then be made on the out-breath. As described in Chapter Three, the breath also moves between the right and left sides of the human System. Thus by this up-and-down and side-to-side movement is built up the spiral pattern of the Caduceus or Staff of Hermes so well known in esoteric

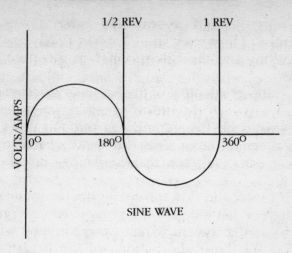

SINE WAVE

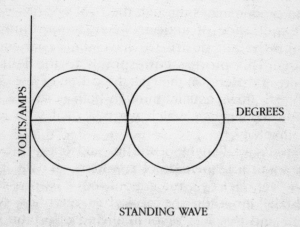

STANDING WAVE

symbolism. When electricity is generated the process can be diagrammatically represented on paper as a sine wave.

By a phase shift of 180° when the impulse reaches its end it returns. Therefore in electrical terms the Caduceus is really just two sine waves going out and returning, called a standing wave. We must remember, however, that this is really in three dimensions and the wave forms are therefore really spirals.

This side-to-side flow of the breath is reflected in the manner in which the breath varies between the right and left nostril. It predominates through one or the other at certain times. This has already been touched on in an earlier chapter (see Alternating Currents, page 30).

By causing the flow of energy to predominate on the right or left side of our system we can produce changes in that system. When we are in tune with the macrocosm these alternations of the breath occur naturally and at the appropriate times. When the breath predominates through the right nostril we have the experience of action. When it predominates through the left nostril we have the experience of sensing. This process corresponds to the Pillars of Severity and Mercy in the Qabalistic Tree of Life. When the breath flows equally through both nostrils it has a special significance which we will deal with in the next chapter.

The relative lengths of the in- and out-breaths and the intermediate periods of retention — both in and out — are also of great importance. It is possible to gradually lengthen the period of retention of the breath and this has a spiritualizing effect on one's consciousness. Conversely lengthening the period during which the breath is held out produces the opposite effect. One notices this principle in sighing. An upward sigh reflects an aspirational mood as, for example, when one experiences a sense of wonder at some breathtakingly beautiful scene. A downward sigh reflects a feeling of lethargy as in yawning when one's energies are flowing downwards.

It is sometimes felt that the ideal is to balance the upward and downward impulses of the life force by an equal rhythm of the in- and out-breath. However, as we have seen, life is a continually changing flow requiring different qualities to manifest at different times. Therefore it seems more logical that we should be able to vary both the upward and downward as well as the left and right rhythms of breath to suit the needs of each moment.

Very few people make the fullest possible use of their potential capacity for breathing. Breath is life and the amount of breath which we can take in is vitally important. Generally, slow breathing will also be deeper breathing, and fast breathing tends to be shallow. Many yogis measure the length of life not by the number of years lived, but by the number of breaths taken. Also there are still many people who have the extremely unhealthy habit of breathing through their mouths.

Regeneration

By emphasizing the in- or upward breath one is spiritualizing or regenerating oneself. Degeneration is emphasizing the down-going breath. And generation is an appropriate rhythm between the two.

This principle has its interesting counterpart in the field of economics where the process of regeneration corresponds to the activity of investment. By investment one forgoes immediate spending in order to create still greater income later on. It is the principle of saving, or waiting. By regeneration one is reinvesting one's energies in order to promote greater soul growth. Degeneration is too much spending. Generation is a balance of spending and saving.

Control of the Breath

The breath takes on the form of the particular tattwa (shown on page 47) which is predominating in the system at any one time. This can be seen by projecting the breath on to a mirror. Recently some scientific research has been done in photographing etheric forms which seems to bear this out.

Patient observation of one's own breathstream eventually leads to the ability to control the vital forces and focus them at will at the different levels. Gradually one learns to recognize the changes in vibration which occur as the breath or life force passes through the different levels. In this way one learns to control the elements or tattwas.

So long as the breath is ebbing and flowing we are living in the world of polarities — the world of form. The ultimate step in control is when the breath is suspended altogether and one leaves the world of form and withdraws into the spiritual realm, the universal consciousness. Only the adept can withdraw completely in this way.

Withdrawal, however, is very much a matter of degree. It is through the same gateway that one passes in sleep, death, or in deep meditation, but only the degree of withdrawal is different.

Sleep

The depth of sleep varies greatly with different people. Some hardly leave the body or sense consciousness during sleep. Others leave the sense consciousness but remain active at the mental level experiencing dream states. Some are able to withdraw from the body and mind and remain at a still higher level from which they return truly refreshed when they awake.

Death

The same principle applies to death where the level to which the soul may reach will depend on its evolutionary progress. Some souls remain practically earthbound even after discarding the physical body. Often they are already seeking to reincarnate or sometimes to experience the sense world again through an incarnate soul whom they may try to influence or possess. Others will pass peacefully to higher states. They may first renew relationships with other discarnate souls and eventually pass to still higher 'summerlands' to renew themselves completely until the impulse to express themselves in form leads them once more to incarnate.

Deep Meditation

In deep meditation one is consciously doing, or

attempting to do, what most people do more or less involuntarily in sleep and death. One is withdrawing to that level within, where one renews oneself at the eternal fountain of life — one's own spiritual source.

This process too is a matter of degree according to proficiency. The adept who has learned to control his breath or life force at all levels is able to suspend it and withdraw from his body, but without abandoning it. He is also able to return to it again when he needs to. By consciously dying at the necessary times in order to renew himself he avoids the need to die involuntarily in the common way.

Such an adept might require a long life span extending perhaps over several centuries in order to complete some important work for the evolution of humanity. Therefore he would retain the same body during that period by renewing himself in this way. This might be especially necessary in view of the difficulty for such a highly evolved soul in finding the suitable circumstances into which he could reincarnate through birth. Such an adept would at the end of a life cycle dematerialize his body when his work at that level was completed.

Life Cycles

The length of one's life is really proportionate to the soul or higher self's motive for living. When the soul has exhausted its purpose it withdraws having used up its downward impulse. A high sense of purpose is derived from spirit, and so when its purpose is exhausted it must renew itself in spirit by withdrawal.

All life manifests in cycles. Each in — and out — breath, each day and night of waking and sleeping, each life and death in a body, these are all the same principle, but operating at a larger or smaller scale. They are all the periodic or cyclic law operating as life vibrates between its poles.

CHAPTER EIGHT

PRACTICE

The science of the chakras is very much the science of *breath* and *posture*. In order to fully appreciate their enormous significance these two terms have to be understood in their widest sense. *Posture* is to be understood as one's total attitude to life at all levels. Therefore one can speak not only of physical but also of mental and spiritual posture. *Breath* is to be understood as the movement of the life force throughout the entire system; as the flow of energy between its poles of spirit and matter.

Bearing these principles in mind and with the knowledge of man's occult anatomy outlined in the first part of this book, the purpose behind the practices of yoga becomes very much clearer.

Preliminaries

Any serious programme or system of self-training has

to begin with attention to the basic rules of health at the simplest levels. These may be compared to the foundations of a house. One may neglect the foundations at first with apparent impunity. But later on when more weight is added to the structure the building will not stand up. The same principle applies to self-training. Building on an insecure foundation means eventually having to go back on one's work to remedy the defects. For as one goes higher in self-training one contacts greater energies and brings these into activity in one's system. If the system is not strong enough it will not be able to contain them. This may be compared to pouring very hot water into a container which has flaws in it and therefore breaks up.

These basic rules are to be found in all the classical systems. Harmlessness to all life, truthfulness, cleanliness, right diet, freedom from excesses in any field — all these qualities are the equivalent of the foundations of our building. A foundation is a basic strength upon which to build and these virtues are in fact strengths of character upon which we can build our higher development.

HATHA YOGA

The next step is the work of balancing the lower energies in the system. Many people do not understand why the Hatha yoga postures and exercises are really necessary in self-development. They try to take a short-cut by omitting the whole of this initial but vital part of the process.

Let us take a simple illustration which makes this point quite clear. If one attempts to balance a pencil upright on its end at first it is necessary to keep steadying it with the hand to prevent it falling over. When it is balanced, however, one can remove one's hand and it will remain upright. Now consider the body as the pencil. The aim of Hatha yoga is to bring the body to such a state of health and perfection that its forces are balanced. Only then can one withdraw one's attention from it and concentrate one's attention at higher levels. In fact so long as the body is not in perfect equilibrium the attention of the mind will be continually absorbed in it in just the same way as the hand's attention was continually absorbed in steadying the pencil until it was balanced.

We have all at some time had the experience of being unable to sleep due to pain in some part of our body. At such times the consciousness is continually absorbed in, and therefore attached, to this pain, so that it is unable to leave the body. When the pain ceases, however, the consciousness can leave it and pass upwards into the sleep state. The whole aim of Hatha yoga is to be found in this analogy. It is to bring the body into such a state of equilibrium that the consciousness can be withdrawn from it and pass upwards to higher states.

In terms of the chakras, Hatha yoga prepares the energies at the lower levels to be raised to the higher ones. When the energies have been so raised the preliminaries are no longer so necessary.

This point is made clear in the classical yoga textbook the *Hatha Yoga Pradipika* which says that the various asanas, bandhas and pranayams should be practised 'so long as Raja Yoga has not been attained'.

71

However, it is also possible to practise Hatha yoga without having much understanding of its real purpose. A great deal of yoga practised both in the West and East falls into this category and has become merely a fashionable new kind of gymnastics. Many people, not realizing that this is a means to a higher goal, make it an end in itself so that it becomes a glamorous kind of acrobatics or contortionism. Of course even with this limited motive the practitioner will still derive benefit to his health but the real purpose will have been missed.

Clearing the Nadis

With a knowledge of man's occult anatomy and a clear idea of the aim of yoga, the purpose of many practices becomes easier to understand. Initially the aim of these practices is to free the posture from any blockages or kinks which may be inhibiting it. Nearly everyone has some blockage at some points in his system: that is to say, there is a resistance at some point to the flow of the energies. In fact all disease is merely a restriction of the flow of the life force in a particular area. In yoga terminology the channels through which the energies flow in the human system are called *nadis*. These nadis have to be cleared of blockages and enlarged. This process is an important part of Hatha yoga. Exercises and postures which involve bending, twisting and stretching the spine fall into this category of generally promoting greater energy flow throughout the system.

Balancing Postures

Another important category of postures is those which promote balance. We have seen that balancing the forces has a vital significance especially when we come to the question of the third force or kundalini. Postures and exercises which train one in the art of balancing are important in learning to control the positive and negative forces in the system and bringing them into equilibrium.

The Lotus Posture

The lotus posture and its variations has a combination of effects. First, it provides a stable triangular base on which the spine and upper part of the body can be supported at ease. This is essential for later stages of meditation and concentration. If correctly performed it also has the effect of causing the spinal column to be held erect on the pelvis. Secondly, by crossing the legs and either joining the hands or placing them on the knees, the open energy circuits are closed. Energy which would normally leave the system through the hands and feet is therefore retained. Slight pressure from the heel on the perineum aids the upward flow of energies from root to crown. Thirdly, this posture is essentially a sublimative one. Through its practice the energies in the system are retained, brought under control, and sublimated up the vertical polarity of the spine to the higher centres.

After the preliminaries a further stage can be reached when certain practices which directly affect the chakras may be undertaken. The subtle effects which various postures, mudras and bandhas have on the energies in the system is an extremely complex and difficult subject. Very few of those who practise yoga seem to understand fully these effects. Some portions relating to this subject are kept secret. However by correlating the explanations of man's occult anatomy already given with his own experiences in practice, the student can work these out for himself to a great extent.

We give certain examples which may serve as guidelines in this field: inverted postures for instance cause the energies to flow upwards to the higher chakras. The comparison of an ordinary electrical battery is helpful here. Current flows between the positive and negative poles. When the battery is discharged the method of recharging is to reverse the flow of current through it between its poles. In the human system by standing on one's head one is doing just the same thing; reversing the flow of energy between the polarities on the vertical axis of the spine.

The student will also readily be able to realize for example that the throat and heart are strongly affected by certain postures. In particular the shoulder stand has a remarkable effect on the throat centre provided that the body is held absolutely erect and at right angles to the neck with the chin pressed firmly against the sternum. Bow postures with the breath retained cause energies to flow into these chakras provided the head is fully held back.

As a further example, certain postures are effective

in activating the solar chakra. These are principally the ones which draw in the abdomen and exercise control over the energies centred there. After practising these correctly one becomes aware of a greatly increased activity of the gastric fire or fire element in the system. Similarly the sacral and root centres are affected by their appropriate postures.

These postures and exercises should always be practised:

(a) With a knowledge of the purpose and effect which they are intended to promote.

(b) Slowly and deliberately without hurry or anxiety.

(c) With complete one-pointed concentration on what is being done.

Kundalini

The best way to understand the mysterious third force or kundalini is by the illustration of the pendulum. When the pendulum is in motion it swings continuously from side to side vibrating between horizontal or right and left poles. It also has a vertical polarity and as it swings, energy is transmitted downwards from its pivot or source. If its motion ceases the right and left poles becomes balanced and cease to exist. Then the energy which was being sent downwards must also return to its source and travels upwards along the pendulum which is now stationary in the middle.

In yoga terminology the right and left side energy flows are *Pingala* and *Ida*, and the central channel is *Shushumna*. In Qabalistic terms they are the Pillars of

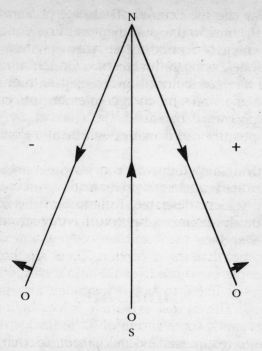

Severity and Mercy and the central channel is the Path of the Arrow. In Buddhism it is the Middle Way; in Chinese terminology the Tao or balance of Yin and Yang; in Christianity the straight and narrow path. Kundalini, therefore, is the path by which the energy returns to its source when it ceases to manifest in the human system as a vibration between poles. When kundalini returns to its source the pendulum has ceased to swing. All polarity ceases and our consciousness returns to its source through the crown chakra. When the breath ceases to flow through the right and left sides of the system either we die or if we have prepared ourselves and the energy is controlled, we can transcend death and can pass consciously into the deep mystical state of *Samadhi*.

There is considerable misunderstanding concerning the awakening of forces in the human system which then, it is said, activate the chakras. On the whole this is putting the cart before the horse; it is truer to say that when the nadis or energy channels are purified, and the forces are balanced, the chakras are ready; then the energies can flow through them and not vice versa.

In all nature forced growth is never the most healthy kind of growth, and sudden dramatic awakenings of forces are seldom desirable. Instances of this kind of unbalanced development seem to have received more publicity than they merit and are often assumed to be the rule rather than the exception. There are, however, certain people in whose lives the awakening of forces or faculties is likely to be very sudden and perhaps unexpected. This is due to karmic forces building up gradually against some strong obstacle or deep-rooted hindrance to that person's development. In such a case the obstacle will go on resisting until the forces building up finally overcome it and as a result a sudden change in the pattern of life and its energy flow comes about.

At a later stage the highly evolved soul learns to control the powerful awakened energies which flow through his system. He will be able to direct them upwards or downwards, or focus them at whatever level he requires. For some people the effect of the sublimation of the awakened kundalini will be one of rejuvenation. One is reminded of Rider Haggard's 'She' who preserved the prime of her body by bathing in the sacred fire in the mountain. It is interesting to speculate how much the author knew of the esoteric aspect of his subject concerning the real sacred fire within.

RAJA YOGA

The Mind

The mind is often compared by yoga teachers to a pond, the surface of which is covered with innumerable ripples caused by the winds of desire blowing upon the water and ruffling it. Only when these winds cease to blow does the water cease to be agitated. Then it becomes calm and lucid and a totally new experience supervenes because it is possible to look down through it and see the bedrock of the pond beneath. Previously, due to the water's agitation, one could not have seen the bedrock of the pond or known that it existed. In this analogy the water of the pond is of course the mind, and its substratum or bedrock is the higher principle within ourselves which is above the mind — the spiritual consciousness. The winds of desire are the emotions which ruffle the mind.

Desire and Emotions

True concentration of the mind is therefore only possible when we can achieve dispassion and detachment from our emotions. We have seen already that thought descends through the etheric level to manifest through the four elements, which are themselves modifications of the ether. Whenever the mind, therefore, is associated with any of the elements it is in a state of emotion. In terms of the chakras, when the energy of the brow chakra begins to take on the vibrations of any of the five lower chakras its own vibration is lowered and it becomes tinged by emotion. Every emotion is an association of the thought principle with one or more of the elements which then colour or condition it. Pure thought, uncoloured by any of the lower vibrations, is the unconditioned mind.

Unconditioned Thought

The unconditioned mind is free from the organs of sensing or acting associated with the lower chakras and is self-contained in its own vibration. Such pure thought is tremendously potent. Faculties such as thought transference, materialization, and mind reading depend upon the ability to concentrate the mind by freeing it in this way. As we have already seen earlier in this chapter the ability to do this depends initially on proper preliminary training at the Hatha yoga level. Thus Hatha yoga leads on to Raja yoga in a natural sequence of progress.

Transcending Thought

Finally the energy of the brow chakra must be raised

to the higher vibratory rate at the crown. This step is only possible and should only be attempted after the mind has been thoroughly disciplined and a high level of mental concentration achieved.

In order to have complete control of any instrument one must be able to take it up, use it efficiently, and lay it down again at will. Only then does it become a true instrument. Only then can one stand back from it and say, 'This is my instrument, it is not me; I am separate from it and I control it.'

The mind has to be trained to this degree before the final stage can be achieved. The thoughts have to be brought under complete control. Only then can we make the subtle distinction between the thought and the thinker. When we realize that *I the thinker exist independently of my thought* we can lay down the thought and remain conscious at the *I am* level alone. Then we cross the final bridge from *Not Self* to *Self*.

Dangers in Practice

Many students are concerned about the possible dangers involved in the practice of yoga, especially if self-taught. Some comment on this question would seem to be appropriate here. First, one should realize that danger is a relative term. What is dangerous for one person may be completely safe for another. Therefore one cannot logically say that anything is dangerous in itself except in relation to the person doing it. Secondly, everything in life that one does carries some element of risk. If there were no risk at all in that activity then the return or results from it would be negligible in creative importance. The reward is always proportionate to the effort involved, and the effort required will be proportionate to the relative danger.

So the whole of life is a process of learning from experiences which when looked back on afterwards appear as mistakes by comparison with our subsequent knowledge. Therefore one needs to be ready to go forward boldly but not rashly into the future ready to improve on what one did before. To take more risk than one can comfortably handle is foolhardy and not to take any risk is equally foolish.

A Guru

Undoubtedly a competent teacher will help one progress more swiftly, but in the matter of finding such a teacher an important point is often overlooked. It is you yourself who in the end has to decide whether or not a certain person is a competent teacher and so the responsibility must finally come back to yourself.

No one can do your learning for you just as no one else can eat your food for you. There will be no progress without a willingness to assume responsibility. In this connection there is a further even more important point, which is that in accordance with the law of karma or cause and effect, one ultimately receives from life what one puts into it. What one gives out and what one receives are two sides of the same coin. However, a great part of humanity has not yet learned this truth which is naturally linked with the law of reincarnation, since the giving out and receiving back is necessarily evened out over more than one life.

This law applies equally to learning in that one may only receive knowledge to the extent that one gives it out. Therefore in order to learn one must also teach what one knows to others who need it. The latter comment involves an important principle of using one's energy in the most economical and therefore most creative way. To give to someone exactly the most useful knowledge that he needs at the moment he needs it is to do this. Trying to force knowledge on people who are not ready for it is a wasteful and therefore an uncreative use of energy. In this, discrimination is necessary to judge whom you can best help, and in which way, and at what time. The door-to-door apostle trying to force his ideas on all and sundry lacks proper discrimination and makes an uneconomical use of energy.

The old adage that when one is ready the teacher will appear is true because you bring yourself by your own efforts into contact with the sources of knowledge which you merit at that time. But even the best teacher can only teach one to teach oneself.

CHAPTER NINE

THE RIGHT USE OF ENERGY

There is a natural tendency to regard any programme of self-improvement as if it were a journey leading to an ultimate destination. This destination is often thought of as final perfection towards which man is continually growing through a process of evolution. It is seen as union with the divine life from which man has become separated and to which he returns along a path of unfoldment.

But although this concept serves a useful purpose for man at a certain stage of his development it has eventually to be superseded by an even higher one. For it is not that the road leads to a final goal, but rather that the road itself is the goal. We tend to represent the journey in terms of space and time as if life came to a stop when we reached a certain point. But really life itself is infinite — it is not static but a dynamic continuum. So that although one needs at a certain stage to think of a goal as an incentive to growth, the end is really endlessness itself.

The idea of life being endless or eternal is something for which most people are not ready. To let oneself go forward into the eternal flow of life without thought of any end is a stage which needs courage and is also a great challenge. This principle helps us greatly where yoga is concerned because yoga too is its own reward. It does not need an end or goal in terms of time. If one's practice makes one more joyful then this is the criterion of progress. Joy is the expansion of consciousness or the principle of 'moreness'. Suffering is the limitation of consciousness, the principle of 'lessness'.

Energy is in Proportion to Motive

Everything in the universe radiates some form of energy, whether it be mineral, vegetable, animal or human. The amount of its radiation is in proportion to its relationship to the total or universal energy. So where the energy system of man is concerned the amount of energy on which he can draw is in exact proportion to the universality or otherwise of his own consciousness. The more selfish and limited his motives in life, the more he shuts himself off from the wholeness of life, and the less the life force will flow through him. In short, energy is in proportion to motive.

Many of us will have had the experience of undertaking some activity in a spirit of fear, hatred, doubt or with some other selfish motive; this always leaves one feeling utterly exhausted. By contrast, those who act with a selfless, universal motive of service and of giving will know that such work brings no tiredness in its wake but in fact brings joy and renewed energy. To the extent that our motive is for the good of the whole, to just that extent do we have the right to draw on the whole or universal energy. In reality life has no shortage or limitation. Energy is limitless and life itself is abundance. It is we who put limitation into life by our finite motives. The measure of a man's greatness or degree of evolution is his capacity for giving.

Nature, it has been said, abhors a vacuum. As we give out energy new life flows in to fill the space. But when we hold back and restrict our creative activity we experience a lack of vital force because we have not allowed the life to flow through us. One may compare this process to that of a water pump which can only receive through its inlet to exactly the same extent that it gives out through its outlet. As we create and receive back we fulfil this law of energy and 'give that we may receive and give again'. Every selfish or limiting action diminishes the flow of life through us; every universal or expanding action increases it.

These principles are often referred to as the laws of universal supply and those who understand and live by them know no shortage but flow joyfully and abundantly through life as a bird flies undoubtingly through the air. Such people make life an adventure — an unending exploration of life's infinite possibilities. This also means of course the infinite possibilities within oneself.

This principle of flowing continuously forward with life's becomingness is symbolized in several age-old parables. There is for example the story of Lot's wife. In the journey away from the city of evil she was turned into a pillar of salt because she looked back. By looking backward one loses the flow of creativity which is essentially a forward-going force and so crystallization sets in. The same principle is symbolized in the story of Orpheus redeeming his beloved from the underworld. He could only save her if he did not look back but kept moving onwards and forwards. As he lost confidence in the future and therefore lost his faith, he looked back and so failed to redeem his imprisoned love or life force.

The Best Use of Energy

Just as water flows downhill following the line of least resistance, so energy always flows to its most useful field of activity. When one field of activity has fulfilled its purpose the life force flows forward into another field. In this way evolution follows a law, for the energy is always moving into that field of activity where it can manifest most creatively. The sum total of energy in the universe does not increase or diminish but is continuously being transformed or transmuted from one state to another. Cessation of activity in one field always means a renewal of activity in another field.

Dharma

This concept of energy flowing to its next most useful task in the evolutionary pattern is embodied in the idea of dharma. Everyone is climbing an evolutionary ladder; therefore in relation to all his circumstances there will be an optimum action for each person at any one time in his life. The next step on the evolutionary ladder for any one person at any one time is his dharma. This is to say that it is the next action into which his energies can best be channelled in order for them to manifest in the most creative possible way.

Control of Energy Through Yoga

The foregoing principles involving the right use of energy are all embodied in the practice of yoga. The flow of life is in fact the breathstream in the human system. The channels through which it flows are the nadis. The different levels at which it manifests are the tattwas. When our flow of creativity seems to dry up then we have to look to the nadis and chakras for the remedy. The breath and posture will somewhere have become blocked. Through yoga one may release the blockages and once more become creative and full of energy. Through yoga we identify our human energies with the universal energies. Just as life itself is infinite and eternal, so our consciousness can become limitless in all its possibilities through yoga.

CHAPTER TEN

ASTROLOGY AND THE CHAKRAS

The relationship between astrology and yoga seems to be only very slightly appreciated. It merits much greater study than it has hitherto enjoyed. There are many aspects of this relationship that are not clear and in which there is enormous scope for further research.

The Flow of All Things

That there is a continual flow of becoming in all life has been understood by both Eastern and Western philosophers throughout the ages. Greek philosophers used the phrase '*II AVTA REI*' (*panta rei*) — 'all things flow'; and Hindu sages used the word *Samsara* — 'the world of becoming'. Astrologers study this flow of becoming through the movement of the planets and heavenly bodies in the zodiac and in its signs and houses.

In general, astrologers see man as being subject to

influences from these planets. Very few astrologers seem to take their science further by enquiring *how* these influences can be effective on the human system. One can easily overlook the fact that any influence can only make itself effective on some object *through a corresponding vibration in that object*. Without such an attunement there can be no rapport or influence between them. It is through the vital centres or chakras that the influences of the planets become effective in the human system.

'As Above So Below'

However, it would be a one-sided view of the subject to look only at the influence of the heavenly bodies on Man's system. Could it not be equally true that the opposite also applies? Each affecting the other? For Man's system of energy flows and his network of chakras is an exact correspondence of the universal system. It is a microcosm of the macrocosm. Can one then say that either affects the other exclusively? It is perhaps truer to say that each is a reflection of the other. The outer and the inner, the above and the below, must both co-exist in reality. One cannot have a top without a bottom or an inside without an outside and so one cannot have a microcosm without a macrocosm.

The Chakra Zodiac

Let us now trace the correspondence between the

outer or astrological zodiac and what we may call the inner or chakra zodiac. The astrological zodiac is formed through the interaction of the higher triplicity or three primary energies and the lower quaternary or four secondary energies as explained previously. The four lower energies we have already seen are the elements. Astrologers term the three primary energies *cardinal*, *mutable*, and *fixed*. Each of the four elements is modified by one of the three primary energies and is therefore in one of three possible states of vibration. Thus is produced a twelve-fold division of the universal system. These twelve divisions of energy have each a predominant characteristic described by symbols or signs with which most students are familiar.

In Man's occult anatomy as we have already seen, the three primary energies have their seats at the three

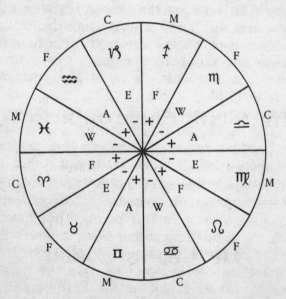

THE COSMIC CLOCK

higher chakras. The four lower chakras are the seats of the four elements. Similarly in the universal zodiac each element is modified by one of the three primary energies, so that it is in either a cardinal, mutable, or fixed state. Therefore, in accordance with this logical sequence, each sign of the zodiac is made up of a relationship between two chakras in Man's system; one from the higher three of the trinity and one from the lower four of the quaternary.

We take for example the sign Taurus. Being of fixed earth we find that its qualities are effective in the human system by a relationship between the throat chakra in the trinity and the root chakra in the quaternary. This would appear to correctly give the extremely fixed characteristic of the sign. If we take the sign Gemini, being mutable air, following the same rules we arrive at a relationship between the brow chakra and the heart chakra. Here again the result appears to correctly produce the extremely mobile and mentally agile quality of this sign.

The Significance of Birth Time

The significance of the time of birth is that it is the point at which we enter the flow of becoming. The flow of manifestation continues, and souls enter it or incarnate into it at various points. The characteristics which are manifesting at that point in time will be the ones which the incarnating soul takes on. It requires these in that life in order to have the experiences necessary for its evolution. We have seen that each experience follows logically from the previous one as the energy flows to its next most useful expression. Therefore from a knowledge of astrology it is possible to predict the future events in any incarnation; even further, the time of future incarnations and under what signs they will be can be predicted.

But when one refers to a knowledge of astrology one means not only a knowledge of the facts upon which it rests, but also the ability to interpret the significance of the data. To record and set down data is the first step, to correctly interpret its meaning and significance is a much greater ability.

The Flow of the Tattwas and the Zodiac

The zodiacal changes correspond to the flow of the tattwas in the human system. Therefore one can read the zodiac and from it see what changes will occur in one's life, or one can determine from the flow of tattwas in one's own system what changes will occur in one's own astrological chart. Yoga at its highest level identifies with astrology. The relationship between the universal breath and human breath can be traced numerically. The universal Zodiac or so-called Platonic Year revolves in 25550 years, giving each sign or age a span of approximately 2145 years. This fact is at present much before the public eye as we leave the Piscean Age and approach the new Aquarian Age. The normal human breath rate of about 18 per minute also gives 25550 breaths in a full day. Furthermore, 25550 days gives a life span of 70 years (the average three score and ten for the Piscean Age). Thus the rate of breath, length of life span and duration of universal Zodiac are all related in one rhythm.

At first sight it may seem difficult to understand that through the interaction of only seven levels of consciousness an infinite variety of experiences is possible. Let us explain this by a musical analogy. Any experience is relative to the previous one. Let us suppose, for example, that one plays the note G after the note A. The experience one has from listening to that note will be different from what it would be if one previously heard the note C. In short the previous event modifies the subsequent experience. Not only does the previous note determine the experience gained by hearing the subsequent one but their relative durations also influence the experience. One C coming after three Gs is a different experience from one G followed by three Cs. Two or more notes played at the same time further varies the experience.

Where colour is concerned the same principle applies. Looking at red after blue gives one a different experience from looking at red after green. The length of time each colour is looked at and the combination of colours further varies the experience. The principle can be carried further because the experience before the previous one also modifies the subsequent experience; so does the one before that and the one before that, *ad infinitum*.

Applying these colour and sound analogies to the chakras (to which they correspond) we see that from our chakra zodiac an infinite variety of experiences is produced.

Planets and Chakras

The planets are the equivalent in the universal system of the chakras in the human system. In effect they are the universal chakras. Therefore there must be correspondences between the planets and the human chakras. The key to this is that the vertical axis of a man's spine corresponds to the 'axis of the solstice' of the zodiac which runs between the sun and the moon with each planet in the sign which it rules.

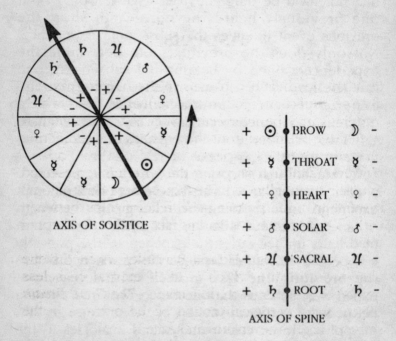

AXIS OF SOLSTICE

+	☉	BROW	☽ −
+	☿	THROAT	☿ −
+	♀	HEART	♀ −
+	♂	SOLAR	♂ −
+	♃	SACRAL	♃ −
+	♄	ROOT	♄ −

AXIS OF SPINE

The revolution of the zodiac corresponds to the descent and return of the breath in its side-to-side wave pattern starting at the brow (there being no polarity at the crown). In this way the planets come opposite to each other in their + and – phases and in the correct order of distance from the sun, starting with Mercury, the nearest and fastest moving, and ending with the furthest and slowest, Saturn. A little analysis will also easily show that the quality of each planet corresponds to that of its relative chakra.

Thus we see the stupendous truth that man is the microcosm of the macrocosm and the real meaning of the ancient adage of the Mystery schools: 'Man know thyself and thou shalt know the Universe.'

Aspects

Relationships between planets in the universal system give us aspects or patterns of influence from which meanings may be interpreted. Similarly, in the human system the relationship of the energies at the different chakras gives us aspects in the chakra zodiac. However, although on paper the system is represented two-dimensionally, it is in fact a three-dimensional system. In understanding the relationships between various parts of the system this fact needs to be kept in mind.

The great occultist Helena Blavatsky wrote: 'Its one absolute attribute which is itself eternal ceaseless motion is called in esoteric parlance *The Great Breath* which is the perpetual motion of the universe in the sense of limitless ever-present space.'

The greath breath is the outer life flowing through the universal zodiac. *The human breath* is the inner life flowing through the chakra zodiac.

The knowledge of the rise and fall of breath comprehends all knowledge.

It is the highest of all sciences.